The Batsford Colour Book of
Dogs

The Batsford Colour Book of

Dogs

Introduced by
BARBARA WOODHOUSE

Colour Photography by Panther Photographic International

B. T. Batsford Ltd · London

Barbara Woodhouse is probably the world's best-known trainer of dogs, becoming renowned for her appearances on television worldwide, which offer a unique blend of warmth, directness, and common-sense. Born in 1910, she was educated at agricultural college, and lived for three years in Argentina, returning to Britain in 1937. She married Dr Michael Woodhouse, and for many years ran a farm, bred and broke in horses, and trained dogs. Two of her dogs, Juno and Junia, became celebrities in their own right through numerous film and television appearances. She has written several books.

Panther Photographic International is run by two partners, Hazel Dodgson and Christina Payne, and specializes in photographing animals. They maintain a huge library of pictures, and have produced work for books, advertisements, calendars and greetings cards. They are active in their local county, Kent, where they provide a portraiture service in animal photography; and in 1981 they won a Kodak Award for Pet Portraiture.

The publishers and the photographers would like to thank the owners of all the dogs shown in this book for their co-operation.

ISBN 0 7134 3726 X

Printed in Hong Kong
for the publishers
B. T. Batsford Ltd
4 Fitzhardinge Street
London W1H 0AH

CONTENTS

INTRODUCTION

Dogs have been a part of human life since prehistory. From the earliest times dogs have been featured, for example, on ancient Egyptian mosaics, and tombs; and when I visited the Ashmolean museum at Oxford, I came upon the stone figure of a dog which, both in size and appearance, was almost exactly like my Great Dane. And that piece of sculpture was done long before Christ was born.

In most countries a man and his dog, or more commonly still a woman and her dog, are a part of the natural pattern of family life, the accepted pattern of the farmer's life, and the existing pattern of the sportsman's life.

Commerce spends millions, and reaps millions, in its dealings connected with dogs.

In show business dog stars often earn as much as their human counterparts. Everyone knows that in a film a dog steals the picture from even the most famous actor, and therefore few actors are willing to accept a part with a canine rival to contend with.

In primitive countries man may depend for his livelihood, or even for his survival, on dogs. The Eskimo knows that his living depends on his dogs. He knows that his dog must be properly trained and conditioned for a working life; few of them are kept as we keep dogs as family pets.

A dog's character is so vastly different from that of a human being, that the words 'my dog is almost human' need careful interpretation, indeed some dogs are so much nicer than some human beings that I am not quite sure the quotation is fair to dogs! What human being if kicked by someone in a temper would not sulk or bear a grudge against the man who committed this crime against his person? Yet a dog will bear no ill will, and at the slightest indication that his master forgives him, whether he has committed a sin or not, will show his delight that he is in favour again.

Dogs must be treated *as* dogs, and to get full enjoyment out of owning a dog you must know what it needs out of life. Take for example a working Collie who is born with the instinct to round up sheep or cattle, and uses his brains, as well as being obedient to whistled or signalled commands; is he happy taken from his natural surroundings and work into an ordinary domestic life of a family, or will his instincts be apt to lead him astray? Isn't this the dog that will chase cars or bicycles simply because in his mind he is herding them as his forefathers did sheep? Is it really kind to expect dogs in one generation to cast aside instinct and be happy walking the streets, doing the shopping, or being exercised in the park? I think not; dogs out of their element often become 'problem dogs', and the owner fails to understand the reason for it, because as far as he knows the dog gets love, good food and daily exercise. But that is not enough. Dogs in the wild state had to hunt for a meal, had to kill to eat or defend themselves. Their senses were highly developed to this end, their instincts were hereditary, and cunning was their companion.

Today, with generations of domesticity many a dog has apparently lost his nose, and uses his eyes instead; he has lost interest in fighting for survival, or if he does possess the fighting instinct to a marked degree his end may quickly be at the vets, and in any case he is a menace to the safety of other dogs and human beings; and cunning is a crime rather than an attribute, so what is a poor dog to do?

Dogs bring out the best or worst in a human being. What is a more wonderful sight than the faithful Guide Dog gently leading his sightless owner on his business, safely negotiating obstacles, ignoring his natural instinct to play or fight with other dogs, yet content to live a rather restricted life in the service of his handicapped owner? This pair belong to each other in a way to be envied by many humans; and all dogs with a real job of work to do come into the same category, when the best is brought out in dog and owner or handler.

No man could cover the mountains and moorlands at the speed of the sheep dog. No machine yet invented could replace that dog. No invention of man can give the companionship a dog can to a lonely person, or an old person, or put up with such infinite patience with rough handling by children in a family. They are outstanding examples of patience and tolerance to be copied.

Let's consider for a minute some of the different roles a dog plays in the world today: they are first and foremost companions, whether they be the humble stray from a lost dogs' home, or the costly show winner. They are part of a home or business, and in these roles receive recognition of no mean standing.

In the home the dog appears in many guises. It may be purely and simply bought as a guard dog, to guard property of value, or just a simple home and its occupants. It may be treated more as a piece of furniture than as an animal with infinite moods, and capable of great love and devotion. The character of that dog is formed according to the treatment it gets, for dogs reflect their owners' character. How often do we hear the words 'he looks exactly like his dog' or 'dogs grow like their owners'? I am quite sure there is much truth in these statements and have noticed that a highly strung nervous owner will have the same defects in her dog, and a placid owner will have a well-adjusted dog.

How often have I seen an old-age pensioner ponderously wending his way along a lane, and a dog equally ponderous wending his way ten paces behind in exactly the same manner? How often have we seen an obviously excitable person with an hysterical yapping dog? For dogs are acutely sensitive to their surroundings, and pick up almost by telepathy their owners' moods and thoughts. My own dogs picked up one of my mannerisms from constantly watching my face for orders or signs of pleasure or displeasure.

Dogs very often play the part of companions or playthings for children. I know in my young days our dogs were a vital part of family life, and I often crept into the kennel with our Alsatian and howled my eyes out on her furry neck. For you can tell a dog what you can't tell a person; the gentle lick of understanding, the look of adoration from deep brown eyes unleashes the pent up emotion; we have no shame with dogs as we have with human beings, for a dog will not tell. To him you can rejoice or cry and there will be no unwelcome come-back; that is why a dog is a true companion. He doesn't let you down, he will listen to you without interrupting for as long as you wish to talk to him. He will not understand all the actual words you are using, only interpret your tone of voice, your mood and your thoughts. If your mood changes he is instantly ready to change his mood too. If you wish to remain sad he will give silent sympathy. Therefore he is the perfect companion for children with all their childish complexes. A dog can be used to further your success in life, to bolster up your ego. What bigger boost to your vanity can you get than a perfectly trained dog faultlessly carrying out your commands in the Obedience show ring, or showing itself to perfection in the beauty ring of a championship show with hundreds of spectators applauding perfection of body or brain? The owner of that dog can reach the heights of exhilaration and achievement, although the dog may not enjoy it.

Take dogs in sport. Greyhound racing is now one of the most popular sports in England and its enthusiastic followers aren't confined to one sex or class. The breeding of the best of these dogs is often done in Ireland, where the dogs have the best of everything as their natural right. I have known households give the best room in their cottage to the housing of their dogs, whilst the family with equanimity occupied second best. The care of the puppies could be a model of infant welfare in the human race, and the exercise and training of value to children instead of dogs.

The training of these dogs is an arduous and long proceeding, under perfect conditions. No dog is allowed to brood alone in a kennel by itself; it has a companion to live with always. Nowadays its health, exercise and training are specialist jobs, mostly carried out by professionals. Occasionally the odd one-and-only pet suddenly rockets to stardom from a small town racing track and brings fame and wealth to its lucky owner. No dogs are catalogued as carefully as Greyhounds, for in a sport or business as lucrative as Greyhound racing the criminal element is always lurking in the background, and the faking of a dog, the doping of a dog, or the substituting of a dog to win or lose a race by design may occur unless stringent precautions are taken. When the puppies are registered, therefore, even the colour of the toe nails is recorded, and it takes a very clever person to deceive the powers that be at the Greyhound Racing Association.

Other sports like hunting and shooting produce different breeds of dogs that for generations have been chosen for their certain ability in the field they are employed in. Beagling, otter hunting, stag hunting, and game shooting all use dogs with natural instincts for their particular type of sport. I well remember tiny pointer puppies not ten weeks old flushing a partridge, standing motionless in a ring around it, with one paw lifted and a quiver in their stiffened tails. Until then I had not fully realised at what an early age dogs knew their job without human guidance.

The sport of the rat pits in North England, long since ended by law, produced the 'Manchester Terrier'; and today its miniature counterpart the 'English Toy Terrier'. These dogs were matched against each other by being put into a pit with hundreds of live rats, and the winner was the dog that killed the greatest number in the shortest time. In one match that took place on March 30th 1847 a dog called 'Tiny', weighing only 5½lb., killed 100 rats in 34 minutes 40 seconds. Even today these little dogs will kill mice in the same way with a flick and a drop, without pausing a second to maul them. In the days of cholera these dogs must have been invaluable to the public health authorities.

Bull-Terriers used to be matched to fight each other, and often pet-owners gather up their toy dogs into their arms when meeting one of these dogs, in case it has designs on their pet. Fox hunting not only provides popular Christmas cards and calendars, but also employment for hundreds of people, as well as sport, and interest in the countryside, not to mention the control of foxes which are vermin in the eyes of the farmers. The hounds are kept differently from the ordinary household pet. They are seldom fed more than three times a week, when they are allowed to gorge themselves on great lumps of horse meat thrown to them. They are not fed the morning of hunting, and this method of management can make it possible for a hound to do possibly over 70 miles in a day. Many of our bigger dogs of the more domesticated breeds are content with three or four miles a day or less exercise, and I can well imagine that even ten miles a day would completely exhaust them.

Hounds are given the taste of domesticity when walked by private households and it must come as a shock to them to change suddenly to a life of strict discipline and work. But it is a great joy to see them greet their previous hosts and to know that even hounds appreciate the kindness of home-life.

Gun dogs are trained with the greatest care, but firmness and strict discipline run hand-in-hand in this training; a gun dog that runs out to game before the command is given is one that is not often in professional circles given many further chances, for the cost of a day's shooting is high these days and the dogs must know their jobs. I have heard of the ruthless shooting of a dog that let its owner down in this way without care or thought that even a dog may err.

A dog's activities can bring out the very worst in a human character, in the show ring hatred and jealousy of a fellow exhibitor, for example; little untruths carefully spread can quickly mar a dog's chance of success in the show world. For the 'dog game' is well known to bring out the worst or the best in dogs and owners. The British are famous, or notorious, the world over for caring more for their dogs than their people. If a dog were imprisoned in a disused mine shaft, there would be dozens of volunteers willing to risk their lives in a rescue attempt, yet children have been known to drown in full view of hundreds of holiday makers without a single person attempting to make a rescue. If an unwanted straydog's story gets into the newspaper, thousands of people write or telephone offering it a home. Few blink an eyelid or read twice the story of an ill-treated child. Yet a dog can be replaced, a child never.

How do dogs react to all this sentimentality from people? Many of them in exactly the opposite way to what we would expect. The dog that receives the adoration and spoiling of an over-sentimental owner very often ends up by biting that owner, or going off on its own pursuits without a backward glance at its home. For dogs need true love, not just sloppy over-sentimentality. They would far rather be trained firmly and fairly reprimanded if need arose, than explained to in a treacly voice how they had hurt their 'loving mummy'. For dogs above all need to respect someone, and that someone should be their owner, and that owner should face up to the fact that dogs are not born good, but are made good or bad by their owners. Dogs do not have human standards for living, and if chastisement is necessary, whether by voice or some other method, it does not have the same effect as it would on a human being. Watch dogs in play, they bite each other unmercifully, roll over, often bump into each other with a frightening thud and enjoy it. Yet if you happen to be training your dog in the street or park and you give it a few corrective jerks, you are almost certain to be threatened by well-meaning but over-sentimental dog lovers who say how cruel you are. One often wonders whether such people would rather see a disobedient dog, and therefore a horrid dog to own, a nuisance to everyone and a pleasure to no one, than have it corrected and properly trained and be a joy to all who come in contact with it.

Owning a dog is one of the best methods I know of making friends. All over the world dogs are a common ground for friendship. It may only be the matching of prowess in some particular field that brings people together, and instantly makes them seek each other's company. It may be the recounting of stories of clever things your dog does. I always used to swear I could talk to almost anyone I wished to by owning a Great Dane and letting it bump into the person concerned, for few people can resist patting these enormous friendly dogs, and having a few words with the owner.

After which the road is wide open for further communication.

I personally met people from all over the world through my own dog *Juno*. We met either because they wished to see her, because she reminded them of a dog they had owned or would like to own, or because a picture of her had appeared in their press, and on visiting Britain they know a dog lover will almost be sure to enjoy meeting his or her counterpart from afar. For there is nothing dog lovers like better than to swap tales or look at each other's photographs of dogs. Even if people no longer own dogs owing to modern restrictions in built-up areas and housing estates, they still possess that inborn love of dogs, and enjoy petting your dog if not their own.

What of the strange people who hate dogs? What of the horrid dogs that hate people? This is not a rare state in either dogs or humans. I remember a woman once at a big dog show rushing past the bench where my dog was, muttering to herself that she hated dogs; and when she stopped to glare at my dog she looked at me and said 'I hate all dogs, they smell'. I didn't bother to tell her that if a dog smells it is the owner's fault, and to hate all dogs for such a trifling reason only showed up the faults in her own character.

I have seen misguided people unwittingly unkind to dogs by forcing their attentions on them, by expecting them to put up with being stroked or having their ears pulled, purely to gratify that person's need for a dog. For a well-trained and beloved dog only wants caresses from its owner, and does not wish for outside love. It does not wag its tail or in any way respond to the stranger, and only refrains from showing its lack of interest because it is a nice dog.

I know people say dogs cause accidents, spread disease, cause people to suffer from asthma on account of an allergy to their hair, tear up carpets, dig holes in gardens, bite owners and tradesmen, spoil beautiful gardens by unclean habits, chase cats, fight other dogs, cause innumerable quarrels between husbands and wives, and occasion hundreds of notices to be put up all over the country with wording such as *'Dogs not admitted'* and *'Beware of the dog'* — yet we still love and own them.

I am aware that dogs are left fortunes in wills. Dogs get mink coats before wives get them. Dogs have research stations devoted entirely to their health and welfare. Dogs now get rare drugs formerly only thought of to save human life. Dogs are discussed by Town Councillors who arrange training for them and their owners in the interest of Road Safety, or supply hitching posts for them in busy shopping areas. Big stores have kennels for them whilst their owners do the shopping. Motoring Associations provide information as to hotels that accept them. A vast number of people are involved with their quarantine and travelling arrangements in the same way as for humans, for the dog is a very important personage, and many a family holiday is made or marred by the presence or absence of the family dog. Without dogs our way of life would be vastly altered.

What is it that a dog asks of its owner? Very little, really. Just a warm place to sleep in its owner's home, food and clean water, sensible training and exercise, and as much fun as fits in with the owner's own life. Respect for its peace and quiet when it is ill or tired, and last but not least a kind end in its own home before its life becomes too much of a burden. This is very often the hardest task for an owner to carry out, and those with weaker characters avoid this duty by giving the dog away to another home when its life of usefulness is nearing an end.

We owe dogs an enormous debt of gratitude, and no book of this kind would be complete without a few words on what dogs have done and are doing for mankind. Let us first look at dogs for their role in war and peace. Nowadays with the modern wonders of detection, defence and criminology, one would hardly think that dogs could still go unchallenged in this field. So far, however, no one has invented a machine with a good sense of smell. The nose of a dog is the most wonderful of all nature's inventions. The tracking by dogs, whether it be of criminals, lost persons, or buried people or in mine detection, is invaluable in the life of a nation in peace or war.

The Air Force, the Army, the Police and security men in factories, all employ dogs to help them in their work. Dogs can pick up scents of intruders long before their handlers have seen or sensed anything. The dog's bark puts terror into any offender, and a dog will attack if his handler is threatened by a gunman, when a human being might hesitate to do so, for dogs do not foresee danger as does a human being. The training of these dogs is so good that the criminal or suspected person does not get injured providing he stands still. But woe betide him if he risks a getaway. For a dog is far fleeter than any man, and even if his scent is hours old over difficult country, a dog trained to tracking can hunt him down. In snow-clad countries where terrible avalanches have buried people, dogs' sensitive noses can find people buried feet-deep in snow, and many lives have thus been saved. Even dogs not belonging to any particular service, just companion dogs, have been known to find their lost owner and lie on the unconscious man's body to keep life in him. Dogs, with their weather-proof coats, are far more fitted to live in rough conditions than human beings; many breeds can swim in rivers and their thick undercoat will hardly be damp. Poodles and Alsatians (or German Shepherd Dogs as they are now officially called) are especially fitted for this, so are Curly-coated Retrievers and Water Spaniels and many other breeds.

In the First World War dogs were used extensively to carry messages between the lines and even to a lesser extent in the Second World War; for dogs could silently pass under wire defences and miss the sentry's eagle eye. The trained dogs became exceedingly clever in avoiding the enemy, reaching their destination with vital messages, or finding the wounded and taking help or messages for them.

In the Malayan War, dogs were a vital part of the Forces' work, for the guerrillas in the jungle sniped at the Forces silently, and the casualties were enormous until dogs were taken on the strength of the army. The dogs were trained to be dropped by parachute and seemed to enjoy it. The handlers and their dogs became inseparable and on return to peace-time many of them were allowed to go home with their handlers as they became redundant in the Forces.

In factories a dog can do the work of a dozen security men, for a dog's keen ears pick up sounds inaudible to men, his nose picks up the scent of an intruder, and his warning bark alerts his handler instantly. His speed when loosed can easily intercept a fleeing intruder.

I believe if dogs accompanied cashiers taking money from banks to business premises, the gangsters would be out of business, for few criminals will face a dog.

One of the most extraordinary things about the nose of a dog and how it works is that there are no hard-and-fast rules about what is the best day or weather or conditions for tracking. Nowadays many amateur dog trainers train their dogs and enter Trials in competition with Police or Army dogs, and it is funny to see perhaps a toy dog do a perfect track in a most unorthodox manner. So many factors vary a scent, such as the wind, the moisture content of the air or of the ground; my own Dane didn't track with her nose to the ground, she did what is termed an 'air track' with her nose in the air. Once she was acting in a film which needed a dog to track someone down, and we dutifully laid a track of liver on the ground, for the director wanted the dog's nose to follow right on the ground, to impress on viewers the fact that the dog was tracking. Of course the dog first of all tracked with her nose about a foot off the ground and victoriously found the liver at the end. This would not do for the film, and in the end we had to drag a sack with some meat in it just out of view of the camera but near enough for the dog to believe she could reach the meat any minute — which kept her nose to the ground.

On the subject of films, I often wonder when I see a finished film how many people realise what skill and patience goes into the working of dogs for movies. Human beings are given hours of rehearsal; no one grumbles at them when they make mistakes in dialogue. But few directors of films look upon dogs as needing practice before shooting the film; they expect them at a moment's notice to do things few dogs do naturally. They seldom remember to praise the dog, but count on it to arrive at the studio at 8 a.m. and stay there bored and hot for hours on end; then, with hardly any warning, carry out difficult instructions with complete strangers, and woe-betide the handler if the first 'take' is not perfect. I feel the training of the dogs is not half so important as a school for directors!

Most film companies, especially where a dog stars, employ more than one dog for the part, as a highly valuable dog cannot do things that involve any risk to itself. Like a human being, it has a 'stand in' who does the boring parts of remaining in one place whilst the scene is lit and the cameras focused. Then the star is called and the action takes place. Dogs play a big part in the success of films they appear in; from the publicity angle studios know which side their bread is buttered, and if possible use shots of the dog as publicity even though it may only appear for a few seconds in a feature film.

Dogs are invaluable when used for charitable purposes. Flag days are sometimes looked upon as a necessary menace now that they are so frequent. Human collectors have a raw time extracting money from people, but put a dog with a box on its back to collect and the money pours in. When collecting with *Juno* my own Dane, I often heard apparently tight-fisted people say: 'Oh, I must give the dog something in her box'.

Dogs on Christmas cards, calendars and chocolate boxes sell like hot cakes, and big business everywhere is seldom slow to take advantage of the popularity of our canine friend. Varieties of dog garments, dog beds, dog beauty preparations, dog foods are almost as numerous as those for humans. Even the dictionary cannot ignore the word 'dog'; I can quickly think of over 50 terms incorporating the word dog, although few have any real connection with the four-legged variety.

You may love dogs, you may hate dogs, but you cannot ignore dogs. Wherever you go, town or country, north, south, east or west, in high or humble society you will meet dogs. Beautiful dogs, ugly dogs, pedigree dogs and dogs of doubtful parentage; clever dogs, stupid dogs, nice dogs, and nasty dogs, brave dogs, and mean dogs, useful dogs and useless dogs. But all dogs just the same. People are kind to dogs, cruel to dogs, there are delightful dogs and delinquent dogs. Whatever they are, wherever you meet them, whatever you think about them, you are bound to know them and this is the reason that this book has come into being. I hope it will give you pleasure, for dogs have been an integral part of my life for sixty years and I don't regret one second of the time spent in their company.

The PLATES

'Remember my waistline!' The Dachshund, which should not be overfed, is a very sporting and sensible little dog suitable for small homes. Very intelligent, he doesn't get in people's way, and due to his small size, he can go anywhere with you. As their name suggests in German, Dachshunds were originally bred to go down holes in chase of badgers; but now they are happy to join in all the family's activities. There are six different varieties of Dachshund — this is a Miniature.

'It's been a hard day!' The English Setter is a sporting breed, although not as active as the Irish Setter. It has a more placid nature, and is more suited to life as a household pet as well as a gundog.

Left
Wire-haired Fox Terriers are always on the alert. Cuddly and lovable now, in six months' time these puppies will be very sporting, and chasing after rats. They should be owned only by people prepared to take the trouble to look after their coats properly.

Above
Titivated and ready for Cruft's. The Lhasa Apso needs a good deal of coat care to be kept beautiful. These dogs are very intelligent, and are well suited to being kept by town-dwellers, or anyone with small premises.

Left
'Anyone for a bout?' Boxers are extremely lively, intelligent and easy to train. The breed originated from crossings between Mastiffs and Bulldogs in Germany. Always full of fun, they make ideal pets, provided they are disciplined when young.

Right
Centrally heated? The Chinese Crested, an ancient breed, is unusual in that it doesn't have a coat; it has hair only on its feet, head and tail. These are loving and intelligent little dogs.

Sporting Basset pups. The natural role of the Basset Hound is to run in packs, chasing hares, although they have been popularized by the advertising for a famous brand of shoes.

Above
Where's that bird gone? English Springer Spaniels are typical sportsmen's dogs, and not domestic pets. Gifted with boundless energy, they are outdoor dogs and should be given work to do. They are not suitable for flat-dwellers.

Right
'I've got it!' Ideal for retrieving in water and rough places, the Curly-coated Retriever has a water-proof coat. He belongs more as a sportman's dog than a family pet, but is loving and easy to train.

Above
Game for anything, even dogs much bigger than himself! Every minute of the day is fun for the West Highland White Terrier, known affectionately as the 'Westie'.

Right
Food, morning, noon and night! The Dalmatian is notorious for being hungry every minute of the day. In smart Victorian society, at least two Dalmatians would have accompanied their owner's carriage. Today these dogs have no real work to do, although with training they are ideal companions for an active owner.

Above

Shampoo and set: with unbelievable patience, the Maltese submits to endless preparation for show. Needing a great deal of care, this breed was developed to look appealing in Milady's Boudoir. The Maltese coat has a beautiful texture — the combings can be spun and made into very high-quality garments.

Left

Reach for the sky! Border Collies are working dogs, capable of covering as much as 40 miles in a day. Gifted with a strong herding instinct, they are not really suitable as pets, tending to get neurotic if not given work to do.

Right

Master's coming! The Borzoi, a very elegant breed, comes from the plains of Russia — now they are found far from their natural surroundings. They are 'sight dogs', like Greyhounds, with the capacity for seeing great distances. Indeed, if they see something moving far away and chase it, they can be difficult to get back unless very well trained.

Left

A popular toy breed, the Cavalier King Charles Spaniel comes in four colour varieties. Cavaliers are ideal pets for everyone in the family; they will walk miles with the more active members, but are happy to stay at home with the less energetic — and so they are suitable for older people, as well as for busy mothers. This breed is not to be confused with the King Charles Spaniel, an older breed so named because of the Stuart King Charles II's fondness for toy spaniels.

Above

Ears upright, like a steeple! This is a Norwich Terrier — not everyone knows the difference between a Norwich and a Norfolk, whose ears fold over. The Norwich is a delightful, sporting little dog game for everything.

Above

Although he really belongs in France, this French Bulldog will be happy as an attractive and loving companion for those who love and take care of him. Great lovers of human companionship, these dogs are not to be confused with the equally appealing Boston, or English Bulldog. They have evolved to be small and highly intelligent.

Right

'Throw that ball!' The toughness and brains of the Welsh Corgi gave him the work in his native Wales of bringing the cattle home to the farm. Silently and swiftly nipping their heels, he is so quick in his movements that no flying hooves can reach him. Corgis still have that propensity, and should not be allowed to worry cattle when in the country. They are easy to train, and make good family dogs — as their Royal connections bear out!

Above
'Not more grooming?' The beautiful Pekingese used to be kept by the Chinese for the killing of mice: now they are favourite pets and show dogs all round the world. They are very intelligent, and if trained do excellent obedience, contrary to many people's expectations.

Right
Ready for racing — Whippets are delightful not only as companions but also in their natural sporting role. They will accommodate themselves to living in towns, but must be given room to move. Due to their slender build, they can be rather inclined to damage their legs.

Beautiful bright eyes: Irish Setters are very active, and extremely good gun-dogs, although they are inclined to end up in the wrong homes. They need plenty of exercise, otherwise they can become easily bored. As shooting dogs, Irish Setters are renowned for their excellent noses. They do not point game, and they are very tender-mouthed. They can be red or red-and-white in colour.

Above
Tug of War! Boston Terriers are full of fun, delightful dogs for any home. One of a number of derivatives of the Bulldog, they will play for hours like this.

Left
'Goodnight: you can do the photography session.' This Lhasa Apso's feline companion is a Blue-cream Longhair. They were brought up together as cats and dogs should be.

Right
Three lovely German Shepherd Dogs. Formerly known as Alsatians, they are known throughout the world for their sagacity and their usefulness to the services and police authorities. They are superb guard-dogs, but need early training to bring out this intelligence to its full extent.

Left

The most beautiful ugly dog in the world. A very ancient breed coming from China, the Shar-Pei has only recently been imported into England, where there are still very few. They are increasingly popular in America, where there is already a specialist club for the breed. By the time he is a year old, the Shar-Pei will have lost most of these gorgeous folds on his body, but will keep them on the head. The Shar-Pei was recently recognized officially by the Kennel Club, and is now qualified in the show ring for Cruft's.

Above

Out for a stroll: almost a rare breed these days, Deerhounds were used in crossings to produce Lurchers, the dogs beloved of gypsies, and now very popular. Very few people have deer to hunt today.

Left
Three's company, four's none. Golden Retrievers are universally loved; they are sporting, easy to train, and good guards. The pups are never too young to learn their first lesson.

Above
'Who's for a chase?' Ready for a walk or a chase after everything in the hedgerow, Jack Russell Terriers make popular sporting dogs — these activities are becoming more frequent all the time.

Above

Who said cats can't be trained (this is a Tortoise-shell Longhair)? The Chow, at any rate, takes very well to obedience training. Originating in China, the Chow has an extraordinary black tongue.

Right

Rescue dog on the Eiger. The saving of lives in snowy conditions is of paramount importance, and the Eskimo Dog is adept at this, sniffing out buried climbers and pulling them to safety on a sled. In this role the Eskimo Dog is not as fast as the Husky, but makes up for that with great stamina.

Left

When he was born, this Pomeranian puppy would have fitted into a tea-cup. Although they are less widely seen than previously, the Pomeranian, or 'Pom', is charming, and makes a delightful pet for the elderly.

Above

'Who's for a day's sport?' Beagles are delightful little dogs to own, full of fun, but not easy to train, being slightly too independent in temperament to take easily to obedience training. The Beagle is a pack dog used for hunting — the skill needed to control these agile little hounds has produced many a fine Master of Fox Hounds in later days. Many famous schools and military establishments run their own private pack of Beagles.

49

This amazing stance is typical of a Pointer — the dog shown is a German Short-haired Pointer. I remember once owning an English Pointer: when her puppies were eight weeks old, they stood, all twelve of them, behind their mother with their tails outstretched and one paw raised pointing a partridge — which shows that this trait is hereditary, not taught.

50

Left

Have me, love me, train me: a delightful little
breed, the Cairn Terrier is always ready for a walk,
and sometimes too ready. They need to be
regularly exercised, or they will become
frustrated. Their ears will always become erect
after teething.

Above

Not an 'Afro' hairdo — this is the natural coat of
the Puli, a Hungarian sheepdog. You should not try
to comb out these curls, which are the dog's
natural protection against the weather.

Above
Churchill chose this breed as a pet — and wisely:
the Pug is intelligent, clever and kind, good with
children and other dogs. This is a sturdy breed,
too, although inclined to snore.

Right
Not a washing-up mop, but a sheepdog. The
Komondor came from Hungary, like the Puli. It
also has the same kind of coat, although it is
somewhat larger. The Komondor is not yet widely
popular in Britain, and should be regarded as a
specialist fanciers' dog — it can get very tired
carrying that coat about.

Left

Guarding sheep? Looking out for wolves? The Leonburger is one of a number of Eastern European sheepdog breeds used for guarding flocks. Sagacious, kind, and good watch-dogs, they are still a fairly rare breed, although growing in popularity.

Above

A Labrador puppy (left) with a Golden Retriever companion. The Labrador often works as the eyes of the blind, and is one of the most popular of all breeds, both as a sportsman's dog, and as a family dog. The police, too, use Labradors — for sniffing out hidden drugs.

Above

Ready for anything! Airedale Terriers are delightful dogs once used extensively by the Police — although in this role they have now been replaced by German Shepherd Dogs. If trained they prove highly intelligent, sporting, and good with children.

Right

'Can't wait to pull a milk cart...' The Bernese Mountain Dog, as its name suggests, is a Swiss breed, and was used over the centuries for deliveries! Although not recommended for homes where space is limited, these are good family dogs, even-tempered and friendly. They are easy to train, too, and the coat is not too long to keep easily in good condition.

'I'd rather be out shooting...' Famous throughout the world for their sporting prowess, Cocker Spaniels, which come in several colours, do need a great deal of care and grooming, especially round the ears. They are therefore unsuited for owners who do not have much time to devote to their dogs. A Cocker Spaniel was Best in Show four times at Cruft's, which is a record.

Right
No worries here about the weather — raincoats can be bought for all breeds, and can make grooming less of a burden in bad weather. Collies don't really need them: they have special coats to protect them against the weather, and it is amazing to see how they can clean themselves up if put in a deep straw litter for a couple of hours. The coat of the Rough Collie needs considerable care and grooming, and so the breed is not suitable as a pet for very busy owners.

Boston Terriers were made really popular as a result of appearances in films in the early 1930s. Excellent companions, they are highly intelligent and have a good temperament, although they are inclined to snore. Bostons are very suitable as pets for people who live in flats, or who do not want to walk long distances.

Right

Listening for command! A vast number of non-pedigree mongrels are kept as household pets, and many people say that they are more intelligent and tougher than pedigree dogs. I don't believe this is so, but they certainly win the hearts of most people who meet them.